# WOOD

Sue Dyson

Consultants: The Timber Research and
Development Association

Wayland

## Titles in this series

Bricks

Glass

Paper

Plastics

Water

Wood

**Cover:** (Main picture) Builders nailing cedar boards on to a house in Massachusetts, USA. (Top right) Wooden logs.

**Editor:** Sarah Doughty

First published in 1991 by
Wayland (Publishers) Ltd
61 Western Road, Hove
East Sussex, BN3 1JD, England

© Copyright 1991 Wayland (Publishers) Ltd

**British Library Cataloguing in Publication Data**
Dyson, Sue
  Wood.
  1. Wood
  I. Title    II. Series
  620.12

ISBN 0 7502 0153 3

Typeset by Dorchester Typesetting Group Ltd
Printed in Italy by G. Canale & C. S.p.A.
Bound in Belgium by Casterman S.A.

# Contents

All the words that appear in
**bold** are explained in the
glossary on page 30.

# What is wood?

Wood is used by people all over the world. It is one of the most important materials we have. It can be used for many different things. Boats, paper, furniture and houses are just some of the things that can be made from wood. Wood is strong, springy, warm to touch, and can be cut into any shape. If it is well looked after, wood can last for hundreds of years.

*A map of the world showing where most of the hardwood and softwood trees grow.*

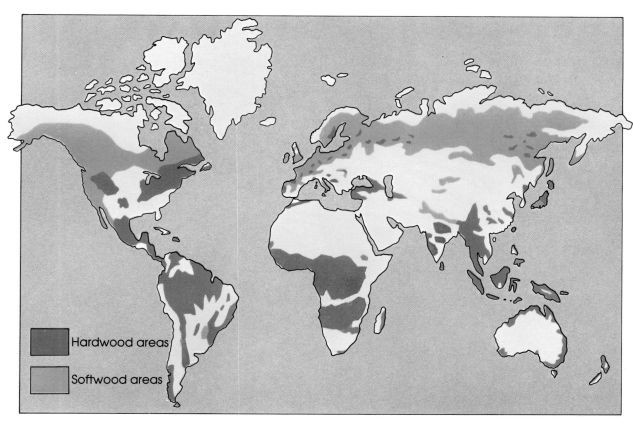

Hardwood areas

Softwood areas

Wood comes from the trunks and branches of trees. Different trees give us different kinds of wood. There are two main types of trees, called **softwoods** and **hardwoods.** But this does not mean that their wood is either hard or soft. Softwood trees have thin, needle-like leaves and carry their seeds in cones. They grow best in countries that have cold, dry **climates.**

Hardwood trees have broad leaves and grow in countries that have mild climates, and in hot, wet places like **tropical rainforests**. Most hardwood trees are deciduous, which means they lose their leaves each autumn.

*A Japanese forest which shows a mixture of hardwood and softwood trees, in autumn.*

5

# Growing trees for wood

Around one-third of the earth's land is covered by forests. But many are being cut down to clear land for farming. Many of the trees in these forests are not being replaced by planting new trees.

Foresters plan and plant forests to provide a steady supply of wood. This means that when trees are cut down, new ones are planted to take their place.

*A forester planting out young saplings.*

*Saplings grown from seed in a Brazilian nursery.*

Foresters grow the trees from seed in **nurseries.** When they are big enough, they are planted outside. At four years old the **saplings** are replanted in the forest or plantation. Both softwood and hardwood trees are grown in plantations. Hardwoods take longer to grow than softwoods.

Each spring, trees grow a new layer of wood. If you look at a tree stump, you will see lots of rings, one inside the other. These rings show each year's new growth. You can count the rings to find out how old the tree is.

*The number of growth rings on a tree stump shows the age of the tree.*

# Cutting down wood

When the trees in the plantation are big enough, they are cut down by **lumberjacks** using motorized chain-saws. This is a very skilled job. The trees must fall in the right place and not damage other trees around them.

Once the trees have been **felled**, their branches are cut off. This makes them easier to transport. The logs are stacked into piles, and loaded by machine on to lorries or trains to go to the **sawmill**. In some countries the logs are floated down the river to the sawmill. On steep slopes helicopters may be used to drag the logs away.

**Above** *A lumber-jack felling a tree with a chain-saw.*

**Below** *These heavy logs are being transported by truck and train.*

Foresters make sure that the right number of trees are cut down. In the tropical rainforests there are no foresters to look after the trees. Millions of rainforest trees are cut down every year and very few are planted in their place. This is why the rainforests are in danger.

*Bundles of logs can be floated downstream to the sawmill.*

# At the sawmill

**Above** *Huge logs are cut into planks at the sawmill.*

The logs are taken to the sawmill where the wood is cut into planks which can then be sold.

When the logs arrive at the sawmill they may be stored in water. This protects the logs and stops them drying out. Then they are fed into a machine which trims off the bark and cuts the logs into planks. Different types of cut can be used to show off the beautiful pattern, or **grain**, of the wood. The planks are then stacked, graded and sorted.

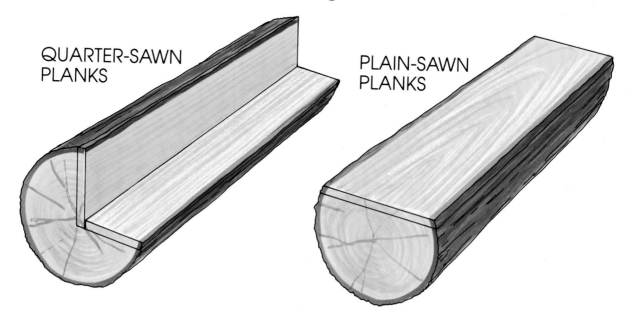

QUARTER-SAWN PLANKS

PLAIN-SAWN PLANKS

*Different ways of sawing logs to give an interesting pattern of grain.*

Freshly-sawn planks cannot be used straight away. This is because the wood has soaked up water and still contains a lot of **sap**. This wood is called 'green timber'. It has to be specially dried out before it is used. Otherwise the wood shrinks, causing it to **warp** and crack.

*Wood seasons slowly out in the open air.*

The process of drying out is called seasoning. Seasoning can be done slowly in the open air, or more quickly in a special type of warm oven called a **kiln**.

11

# Different kinds of wood

You can tell different kinds of wood from their grain. The grain is the pattern of tiny parallel lines you can see on a plank of wood. If the lines are close together the wood is 'close-grained'. If they are wider apart it is 'open-grained'.

Different types of wood are used for different jobs. Many softwoods, like pine and spruce are open-grained. They are cheaper to buy and more common than close-grained hardwoods. Softwoods are used to make everyday objects like kitchen furniture, shelves and floorboards.

*A close-up view of a hardwood and a softwood. What differences can you see?*

SOFTWOOD

e.g. pine

HARDWOOD

e.g. mahogany

| HARDWOODS | Typical appearance |
|---|---|
| Balsa: A lightweight wood which is used for insulation and model-making.<br><br>Beech: Strong, easy to work and used for tools, furniture, gym equipment and flooring.<br><br>Oak: Hard and strong, used for furniture, panelling, shipbuilding, coffins and fencing.<br><br>Teak: A hard-wearing wood, used for furniture, chests and boxes, and shipbuilding.<br><br>Walnut: Polishes well, used for cabinet-making, panelling and furniture. |  |
| SOFTWOODS | |
| Cedar: Lightweight, used for panelling, fencing and roof covering.<br><br>Cypress: Does not easily decay, used for flooring and building.<br><br>Larch: Strong and heavy, used for boat building and fencing.<br><br>Pines: Easy to work and carve, used for furniture, panelling, boxes, buildings, fencing and railway sleepers.<br><br>Spruces: Easy to work and used for ladders, oars, kitchen cabinets, musical instruments and buildings. |  |

Many hardwoods, like mahogany and ebony are close-grained. Some hardwoods take hundreds of years to grow and are very expensive. They can be made into furniture which lasts for many years. Furniture is also made from cheaper woods like pine, and covered with a sheet of expensive wood called a veneer.

*Some common hardwood and softwood trees and their uses.*

# Wood as fuel

**Above** *A Lapp using wood as fuel.*

Wood is a very important **fuel**. More than half of the 3 billion tonnes of wood cut down each year is burned to light and heat people's homes.

If you use coal as a fuel in your home, you are still using wood. This is because coal is made from wood. Millions of years ago, tropical swamps and forests covered the earth. When the trees died, they fell into the swamps and were preserved. In time, the trees **fossilized** and turned into coal.

*Making charcoal in Brazil. The wood is burned under mounds of earth.*

Another type of fuel made from wood is charcoal. Charcoal is made by burning wood very slowly in ovens, under huge mounds of earth. Perhaps you use charcoal at home on a barbecue.

Using too much wood and coal as fuel may be harmful to our planet. When they are burned they produce a gas called carbon dioxide. This is one of the gases in the **atmosphere** that traps heat from the sun. Producing too many of these gases means that too much heat is trapped in the atmosphere. This is sometimes called the 'greenhouse effect'.

*Burning wood, coal or oil releases gases. These greenhouse gases may trap the sun's heat in the atmosphere, making our planet hotter.*

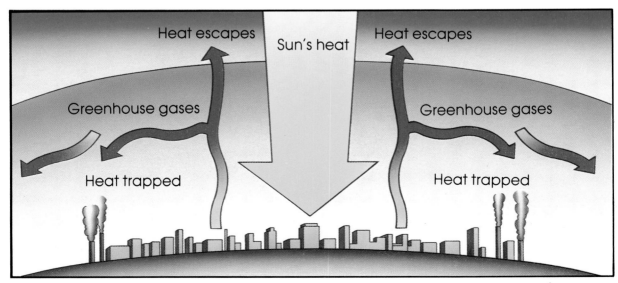

Heat escapes    Sun's heat    Heat escapes

Greenhouse gases    Greenhouse gases

Heat trapped    Heat trapped

# Using up waste wood

All wood is valuable. Even the smallest logs and sawdust can be made into useful products.

Small logs are stripped and chopped up into wood chips. These can be mixed with chemicals to make wood pulp. Wood pulp is used to make paper.

Blockboard is made up of blocks of wood which are glued together. These glued blocks are then sandwiched between thin slices of veneer.

*This machine in Peru is used to make sheets of veneer for plywood.*

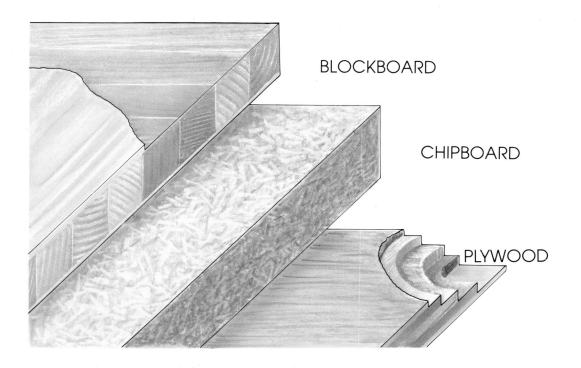

BLOCKBOARD

CHIPBOARD

PLYWOOD

Chipboard is made of wood chips and sawdust. They are mixed with a special glue, then pressed together very hard. When the glue dries it makes a tough, strong material which can be used just like a plank of wood.

*Three ways that waste wood can be made into useful materials.*

Plywood is a sandwich of thin slices of wood or veneer glued together. The veneers are laid down so that the grain of each slice of veneer lies in a different direction. This makes the material stronger and stops it from warping. Plywood is useful in the building industry.

# Chemicals from wood

Wood contains many chemicals which can be separated from the rest of the wood.

Some pine trees contain chemicals such as **turpentine**, and a sticky substance called resin. Violin players rub resin on to the bows of their violins because its stickiness helps to make a good sound. Gymnasts rub resin – a powder, on to their hands to help them grip the bars and ropes.

*Pine trees are cut to collect the sticky resin.*

*Creosote preserves wood so that it lasts for many years.*

Resin is also used in varnish, paint and paper-making.

By heating wood, other chemicals can be taken from it, such as tar, oil, wood alcohol (methylated spirit) and creosote. The oil from wood is used to make **disinfectants**, and creosote can be painted on wood to preserve it. When the wood has been burned, charcoal and ash are left behind. Charcoal is a material which artists use for drawing. The ash makes a good **fertilizer**.

# Wood and paper

We would find it very difficult to live without paper and card. Shopkeepers would have no paper bags or boxes, pupils would have no notepads, and there would be no books, newspapers or comics.

*A diagram showing how wood chips are pulped and pressed to make paper which is then put on to reels.*

Most paper comes from softwood trees that have been specially grown for the paper industry. When the trees are cut down they are turned into tiny wood chips. These are ground up and mixed with chemicals to form

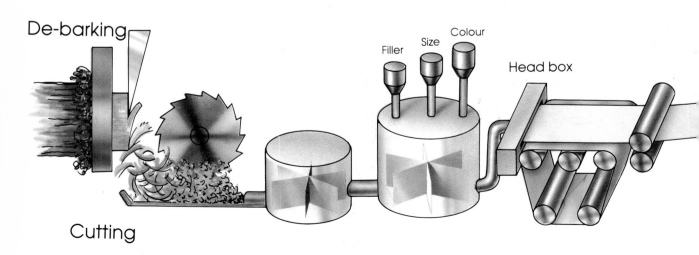

De-barking

Cutting

Filler

Size

Colour

Head box

Mechanical pulping

Chemical pulping

Mixing

Wire-mesh web

a wet, sludgy wood pulp. The pulp contains lots of tiny wood **fibres**. These are squashed together to form the paper. Some of the wood pulp used to make paper comes from waste wood from the sawmill.

The wood pulp is fed into a machine which squeezes it between rollers, to get rid of the water and press all the fibres together. As it passes through the rollers, it gets drier and firmer. At the other end it is ready to be wound into a huge roll of finished paper. Cardboard is made in the same way.

**Above** *Finished paper being wound on to enormous reels.*

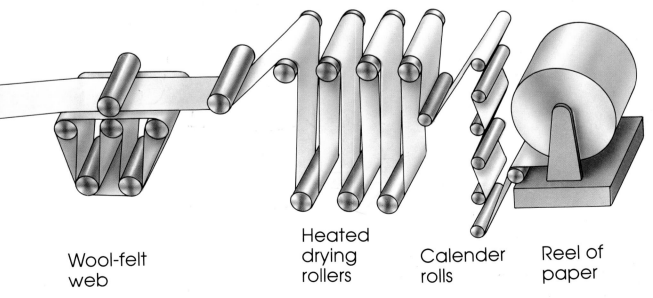

Wool-felt web

Heated drying rollers

Calender rolls

Reel of paper

# Building homes with wood

Wood is the oldest building material in the world, and is still very popular. Wood is easy to cut and use, and is both strong and long lasting if it is cared for properly.

In North America the early pioneers built log cabins by laying logs one on top of another and filling the gaps with clay to keep out the wind and rain. This method of building used large amounts of **timber**.

**Above** *A traditional log house being built in Canada.*

**Right** *Weatherboarding being fixed across the outside walls of a house in the USA.*

*The framework of houses are often made of wood.*

In Australia, Scandinavia and in many parts of the USA timber houses are built using wood planks. Large timbers are used to build the frame of the house. This is then covered with weatherboarding. This wood is coated with wood preservative, paint or varnish to protect it from the weather.

Most houses that are built of other materials still have wood in them. Houses often have timber frames, and floorboards, doors and window frames are usually made of wood.

# Rainforests

Half the trees that grow on earth grow in the tropical rainforests. Rainforests grow in a green band round the Equator. They are needed for life on earth because they clean the air and help to control the world's climate. But the rainforests are in great danger.

*Cutting down the Brazilian rainforest. Once destroyed, the trees will not grow back again.*

Rainforest trees are being cut down and not replaced.

*A group of people in Australia trying to save the rainforests.*

The trees are sold for their valuable wood, or burned to clear land to grow crops or graze cattle. Many plants and animals that live in the rainforests die when the area is destroyed. The land that is cleared for farming does not stay **fertile** for very long. With no trees to protect it, the land quickly becomes **barren** and the soil may be washed away.

*Unless we stop destroying the rainforest, much of it will be lost by the year 2000.*

Every two-and-a-half minutes one square kilometre of rainforest is destroyed. If this keeps on happening, all the rainforest will be gone in fifty years' time. People should know about the value of the rainforests, and **campaign** to save them.

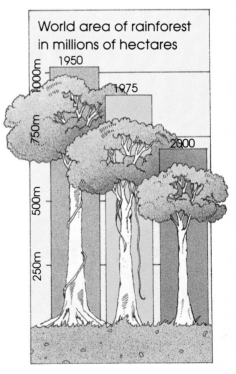

World area of rainforest in millions of hectares
1950
1975
2000
1000m
750m
500m
250m

25

# Recycling paper

**Above** *Waste paper arriving at the recycling plant.*

**Recycling** paper can help to protect our forests. Although many softwood trees are grown to use for paper and new trees are planted in their place, we could save energy by recycling the tonnes of paper we throw away each year.

Waste paper can easily be recycled to make good-quality new paper. The paper is cut into little bits and put into a machine

*The paper to be recycled is pulped with hot water and chemicals.*

called a pulper. Here it is mixed with hot water and chemicals. The chemicals help get rid of the ink, which would make the new paper look grey and dirty. Sometimes the pulp is bleached to make it whiter. You can also recycle paper by simply pulping waste paper with water.

*Finally the pulp is turned into a roll of recycled paper.*

Experts think that we could stop around 35 million trees being cut down each year if we recycled three-quarters of our paper and card.

# Projects with wood

## Make a wooden boat

You will need:

Wood offcuts
A saw
Sandpaper
Glue

One or two corks
A matchstick
A paper flag
Waterproof paints and pens

1. Draw the outline of your boat on to the wood. Ask an adult to help you cut it out with a saw. Sandpaper it carefully until it is smooth.

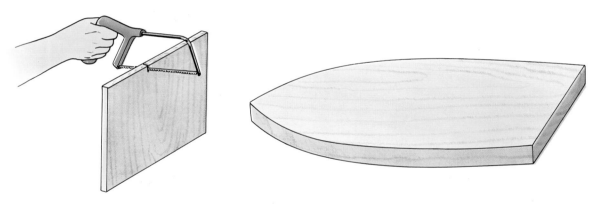

2. Glue the corks on to look like funnels. Glue your paper flag to the matchstick. Make a hole in one of the corks and push in the matchstick.

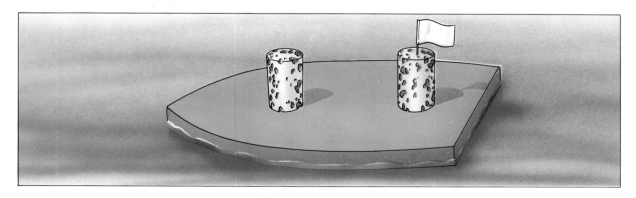

3. Decorate your boat with paints and markers. Varnish it to make it waterproof. Now you and your friends can have a race!

## Make a log cabin

You will need:

Sticks of wood
A craft knife
Glue

Gummed paper
Cardboard

1. With an adult to help you, cut half your sticks to about 12 cm in length, and the other half to about 6 cm. Make a notch on either side of every stick, a little way in from each end.

2. Lay down two long sticks, one for the front, and one for the back of the cabin and glue them to your cardboard base. Lay two short sticks across the sides, gluing the notches together.

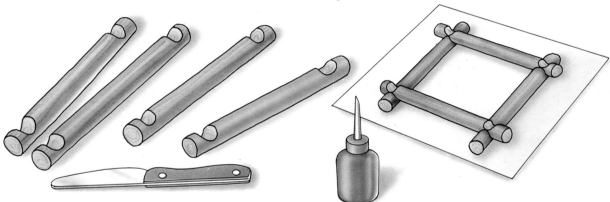

3. Keep building up the walls until they are as high as you want them to be. Glue the sticks together as you are building.

4. Cut out a rectangle of cardboard and bend it in the middle to make the roof. Cut out the shapes for the door and windows from gummed paper and stick them in place.

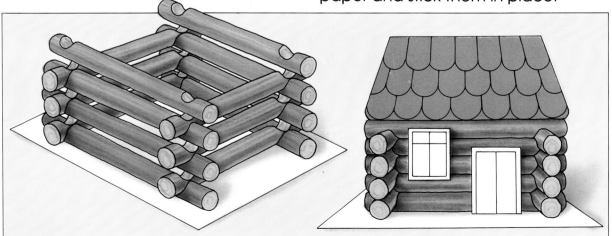

# Glossary

**Atmosphere**   The air that surrounds the earth.

**Barren**   A place is barren if plants and trees are not able to grow there.

**Campaign**   To take action for a purpose.

**Climate**   The usual weather of a particular place.

**Disinfectant**   A chemical substance which kills germs.

**Felled**   Cut or knocked down.

**Fertile**   Fertile land is rich and good for growing crops.

**Fertilizer**   A substance that is spread on land to make plants grow better.

**Fibre**   A long thread, made of cells, found in trees and other plants.

**Fossilized**   When a plant (or animal) has been in the ground for millions of years and has become hard like rock.

**Fuel**   Anything that is burned to give off heat.

**Grain**   The lengthwise pattern on the wood made up by the fibres.

**Hardwood**   A type of tree with broad leaves. Most hardwoods are deciduous, which means they lose their leaves in autumn.

**Kiln**   An oven for drying wood.

**Lumberjack**   A person who fells trees.

**Nursery**   A place where trees are grown from seed.

**Recycling**   When materials that have been used before are treated so that they can be used again.

**Sap**   The juice, largely water, that flows through a plant.

**Sapling**   A young tree.

**Sawmill**   A place where timber is cut into planks.

**Softwood**   A type of tree with thin, needle-like leaves which carries its seeds in cones. Most softwood trees are evergreen which means they keep their leaves all year round.

**Timber**   Wood used for building.

**Tropical rainforest**   The thick forests found near the Equator, where the hot sun and heavy rainfall provides perfect conditions for trees and undergrowth to grow.

**Turpentine**   A kind of oil that comes from trees which can be used for cleaning paint brushes, or thinning paint.

**Warp**   To bend. Wood warps if it is dried out too quickly.

# Books to read

Carrick, G. **Wood** (Craft Projects series, Wayland, 1989)

Chinery, M. **Woodlands** (Kingfisher, 1985)

Jennings, T. **Wood** (A & C Black, 1989)

Keith, G. **Things to do with Wood** (Macdonald Educational, 1980)

Stewart, A. **The Forester** (Hamilton, 1986)

Whyman, K. **Wood** (Franklin Watts, 1987)

## Useful addresses

### Australia
Conservation, Forestry and Lands
    Department
240 Victoria Parade
East Melbourne
VIC.3002

Greenpeace (Australia)
310 Angas Street
Adelaide 5000

### Canada
Canadian Lumbermen's Association
27 Goldburn Avenue
Ottawa, Ontario
K1N 8C7

Forestry Canada (HQ)
Ottawa, Ontario
K1A 1GB

### UK
Friends of the Earth
26-28 Underwood Street
N1 7JQ

Tree Council
Room 101
Agriculture House
Knightsbridge
London SW1X 7NJ

World Forest Campaign
6 Glebe Street
Oxford OX4 1DG

### USA
Greenpeace (USA)
1611 Connecticut Avenue N.W
Washington DC 2009

# Index

## Picture acknowledgements

The publishers would like to thank the following for allowing their photographs to be reproduced in this book: J. Allan Cash Ltd *cover* (top), 11; Bruce Coleman Ltd (John Anthony) 18; Environmental Picture Library 26 (both), 27; Chris Fairclough Colour Library *cover* (bottom), 19, 22 (top); Forestry Commission 6, 8 (top); the Hutchison Library 7 (top), 10; Marion Morrison 16; Photri 22 (bottom), 23; Tony Stone Worldwide 5, 8 (bottom), 24; Wayland Picture Library *title page*, 25; Zefa 7 (bottom), 9, 14 (both), 21. Artwork by the Hayward Art Group 13, 15; Janos Marffi 4, 10, 12, 17, 20-21, 28-29, Elsa Godfrey 25.